Essential Science

Changing Sounds

Peter Riley

W
FRANKLIN WATTS
LONDON·SYDNEY

First published in 2006 by Franklin Watts
338 Euston Road, London NW1 3BH

Franklin Watts Australia
Hachette Children's Books
Level 17/207 Kent Street, Sydney NSW 2000

Editor: Rachel Tonkin
Designer: Proof Books
Picture researcher: Diana Morris

Picture Credits:
Aero Graphics/Corbis: 27t; Oliver Benn/Stone/Getty Images: 20c;
Andrew Brookes/Corbis: 10b; Kevin Flemming/Corbis: 21c;
Greenshoots Communications/Alamy: 5; Kauko Helavno/Image Bank/Getty
Images: 9c; Frank Herholdt/Getty Images: 4, 28cl; ITAR-TASS: 16tr;
Frans Lemmens/zefa/Corbis: 23; Craig Lovell/Corbis: 24b;
Punch/Topfoto: 3t, 15cl; Teisuke Shimoda/Amana Images/Getty Images:
22b; Jim Sugar/Corbis: 19c; Stuart Westmorland/Corbis: 9t;
Woodmansterne/Topfoto: 11c; Michael S. Yamashita/Corbis: 16bl.

All other images: Andy Crawford

With thanks to our models: Josie Cook and Tiaki Losa

A CIP catalogue record for this book
is available from the British Library

ISBN-10: 07496 6444 4
ISBN-13: 978 07496 6444 2

Dewey Classification: 534

Printed in China

Franklin Watts is a division of Hachette Children's Books.

CONTENTS

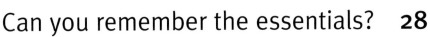

CHANGING SOUNDS

Listen! What can you hear? Keep listening. What other sounds can you hear? Our world is full of sounds but how are they made? How do they travel? How do we hear them? And what really is a sound? In this book you can find out all about sound.

There are many different sources of sound at carnival time. What could be making sounds in this picture?

Volume and pitch

If you look at this picture of a carnival, you can imagine the sounds – the loud music as the crowd passes by, quieter sounds when the crowd has gone, the high squeaks of the trumpets. Notice that we have already started to think about the properties of sound. Loudness and quietness describe the amount or volume of sound that reaches our ears. High and low describe what is called the pitch of sounds.

Sound and distance

If you stand next to someone, you can talk to them in a quiet voice, but what happens if you are 50 metres away? You have to shout! This is because sound becomes weaker as it travels away from where it is made. Look at the picture of the motor bikes. Imagine the engines revving up with a high-pitched sound then the bikes racing away from you. How would the sound change?

It would become quieter and quieter as the bikes ride away into the distance.

The noise from the engines is loud when the bikes are close, but it gets quieter as the bikes speed away.

Data

When scientists do experiments, they make observations and record them. This information is called data. It may be in the form of a table, bar chart or line graph. Collect some data about different sounds by trying this activity.

Listen to the sounds around you for one minute every five minutes. Make a note of the number of sounds you hear that are produced by machines, voices, animals or the weather. How does your data compare? You will find data on many pages in this book. Answers to the questions on the data are on page 31.

Sound source	Time when heard (mins)						
	0	5	10	15	20	25	30
Machines	1		4				
Voices	8	10	2				
Animals				1		1	2
Weather			1	1		1	1

WHAT IS SOUND?

When something vibrates, it quickly moves from side to side or up and down. As a vibrating object moves it pushes and pulls on the material around it, such as air or water, and makes it vibrate, too.

The rice grains jump up and down as the drum skin vibrates.

Feeling and seeing vibrations

If you hit a cymbal with a stick and then touch it gently, you can feel the cymbal tingle as it vibrates. If you press on the cymbal with finger and thumb you stop the vibration – and the sound. A drum skin vibrates, too, when it is struck with a stick but the vibration is difficult to feel. You can see the effect of a vibrating drum if you put rice on it and then hit it. The rice is thrown into the air as the drum skin vibrates.

The cause of sound

A sound is made when something vibrates. This can easily be seen by twanging a ruler on the edge of a table. The ruler moves up and down as it vibrates and makes the air around it vibrate, too. The vibrating air carries the sound to our ears.

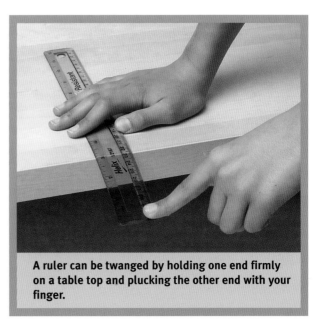

A ruler can be twanged by holding one end firmly on a table top and plucking the other end with your finger.

The tuning fork and water

A tuning fork is a metal object with two prongs called tines. When it is struck, the tines vibrate and produce a musical note. If a tuning fork is struck and the tines are held near water, the surface of the water ripples. The ripples travel outwards from the fork. As they move out across the water, their height decreases and eventually they seem to fade away into the water's surface. This experiment shows that a vibrating object produces waves in the material around it.

The ripples are made by the vibrating tines of the tuning fork.

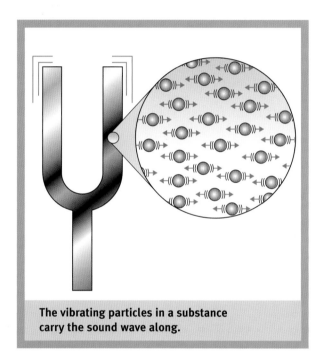

The vibrating particles in a substance carry the sound wave along.

What makes the waves?

When the tines of the tuning fork are struck, they vibrate and push on the air around them. The air is made from tiny particles that can only be seen by a very powerful microscope. The vibrating tuning fork causes the particles to swing backwards and forwards and make the wave of sound that passes through the air.

Rising rice

The table shows how high grains of rice jumped when a drum was hit three times.

1 On which hit did the drum vibrate the most?
2 On which hit did the drum vibrate the least?
3 Which hit do you think made the loudest sound?

Hit	Height (mm)
A	3
B	1
C	5

SOUND ON THE MOVE

If you play loud music, you fill the air with sound. But what happens when you go outside and close the door? You can still hear the music. This means that sound does not only travel through the air, it also travels through solids like doors and walls. Sound travels through water, too.

Spoon test

Bang two spoons together in air and then in a bowl of water. Put them in an empty box and shake it. Listen for the spoons clinking together. You will hear the spoons in each part of the experiment showing that sound travels through air, water and solids.

The string telephone

The string telephone shows that sounds pass through solids. You can make one to test this. Thread one end of a long piece of string through a hole in the bottom of a plastic cup. Do the same with the other end with another cup. Pull the string tight between the cups. If you talk into one cup, your friend can hear you speaking in the other cup because vibrations made by your voice pass along the string.

The string telephone does not work if the string is slack. It must be tight so the vibrations can pass along it.

Singing whales

Whales make a wide range of sounds from groans to trills. These sounds pass through the water and can travel for hundreds of kilometres. Scientists think that the sounds are used as a kind of language but are not sure what the sounds mean.

Whales send sounds to each other through the water. The sounds are known as songs.

An exploding star is called a supernova. It makes no sound in space as sound does not travel through a vacuum.

Silent space

We know that sound can travel through air because it is made from particles of gas that vibrate. In much of space there are no gases. The empty space is called a vacuum. Sound cannot travel across a vacuum. This means that space is silent. If you were in space you would not hear anything even if a star blew up.

Speed of sound

You can find out more about the speed of sound on page 26. The table here shows the speed of sound in a solid, a liquid and a gas. It is measured in metres per second.

1 How does the speed of sound change when it moves from air to water?

2 How much faster does sound travel when it moves from water to steel?

Material	Speed of sound in m/sec
Air	343
Water	1,500
Steel	6,000

SOUND WAVES

We have learnt that vibrations make sound waves. Let's look more closely at them.

The parts of a wave

A sound wave has four parts: the top or crest; the bottom or trough; the wave height or amplitude; and the wavelength, which is the distance between two crests or two troughs. The four parts of a wave affect the sounds we hear.

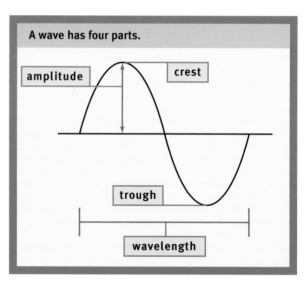

A wave has four parts.

amplitude | crest | trough | wavelength

Echoes

If you watch waves crashing against the seashore, you see that they do not stop but turn round and go back out to sea. They are reflected. The reflected waves are smaller than those which hit the shore because some energy has been lost to the shore. Sound waves behave in a similar way when they strike a surface. Some energy is absorbed and smaller waves are reflected. Usually we do not hear sounds from reflected waves but in certain conditions we can. These sounds are called echoes.

Sound waves on a screen

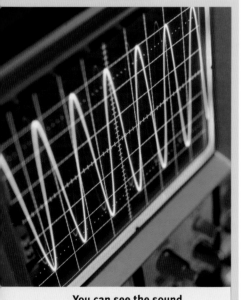

You can see the sound waves on the screen of the oscilloscope.

We cannot see sound waves but a device called an oscilloscope makes them visible. A microphone is attached to the oscilloscope. When sound waves reach the microphone they make a part of it vibrate and produce small electrical currents. These travel along a wire to the oscilloscope where they are used to make a picture of the wave on a screen. Scientists use oscilloscopes in many experiments on sound.

Why sounds die away

A vibrating object creates energy as it moves. This energy passes to the particles in the material around it as it pushes on them. The particles swing backwards and forwards and push on particles further away from the vibrating object. As they do so, they use up some energy so they push with less force than the vibrating object. This means that as you move further away from the vibrating object the height of the sound wave becomes smaller and smaller. When all the energy is used up, the sound wave stops and you can no longer hear anything.

Sound waves are reflected from any surface that they strike, like waves hitting the seashore.

Wave height

The table shows the heights of waves in mm as they move away from a sound source.

1 Which wave increases in height as it moves away?
2 Which wave stays the same height?
3 Which wave decreases in height?
4 Which wave shows the way sound waves really change?

	Wave distance in mm					
	0	10	20	30	40	50
A	5	6	7	8	9	10
B	5	4	3	2	1	0
C	5	5	5	5	5	5

LOUD AND QUIET SOUNDS

Thunder rolling through the clouds, wind roaring in the trees and aircraft taking off all produce loud sounds. The purring of a cat or flicking through the pages of this book are quiet sounds. The difference between them is the amount of energy they carry. Loud sounds have higher waves than quiet sounds.

When you shout, the sound has higher waves than a quiet sound.

When you whisper, the sound has lower waves than a loud sound.

Sounds and energy

You can feel the amount of energy used to produce quiet and loud sounds with a simple experiment. SHOUT THESE WORDS. Now whisper these words. You hardly use any energy when you whisper but you use a great deal of energy when you shout!

Height of waves

When an object vibrates, it moves quickly backwards and forwards and makes the particles around it swing backwards and forwards, too. The moving particles produce the sound wave. If the vibrating object has a great deal of energy, it makes large movements as it vibrates and this makes the particles take long swings as they move backwards and forwards. This in turn makes the height of the sound waves large, too, and the sound is loud. If the vibrating object has only a little energy, it makes small movements as it vibrates and this makes the particles take short swings as they move backwards and forwards. This, in turn, makes the height of the sound waves small and a quiet sound is produced.

The scale of loudness

The loudness of sounds is measured in units called decibels (dB). We can just about hear sounds of 10 dB while sounds of 160 dB would permanently damage our ears. The decibel scale is an unusual scale. A sound of 20 dB is not twice as loud as a sound of 10 dB but ten times as loud. This means a sound of 30 dB is a hundred times louder than a sound of 10 dB, and a sound of 40 dB is a thousand times louder!

The sound of people taking measures about 50 dB on the scale.

The decibel scale

Here are some everyday sounds on the decibel scale. Sounds become painful at 130 dB and cause permanent damage to your ears at 160 dB.

Sound	Loudness in dB
Jet aircraft taking off	130
Road drill	110
Someone shouting	100
A vacuum cleaner	80
A busy street	70
A busy department store	60
People talking	50
A quiet street	40
A whisper	30
In library	20
A pin drop	10
Limit of human hearing	0

How does the loudness of sound change around you?

Construct a table like this one and fill it in at different times of the day. Use the decibel scale on this page to help you estimate the loudness of the sounds you hear.

How does the loudness of sounds around you change throughout the day?

Time	Source of sound	Estimated dB
8.00am	cars	70
10.00am	people	50
Noon	busy café	60
2.00pm		
4.00pm		
6.00pm		

THE EAR

The ear receives sound waves and changes them into tiny electrical currents which travel on nerves to the brain and give us the sensation of hearing.

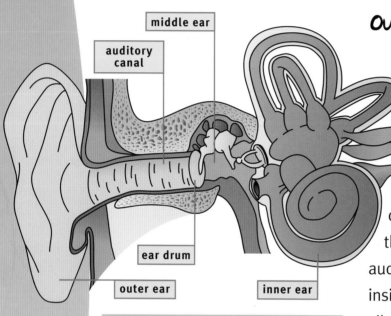

middle ear

auditory canal

ear drum

outer ear

inner ear

The ear is divided into three parts: the outer, middle and inner ear.

Outer ear

The outer ear is made up of the pinna (which we just call the ear), made of skin and cartilage, a tube called the auditory canal and a thin layer called the eardrum. The pinna collects sound waves and directs them to the auditory canal. The auditory canal directs the sound waves inside the head. The eardrum sets up vibrations inside the head when the sound waves reach it.

The middle ear

Three tiny bones in the middle ear transfer the vibrations of the eardrum to the inner ear. The vibrations of the eardrum are too weak for the inner ear to detect them so as they move through the bones, the bones are connected in a special way that makes the vibrations stronger. This allows the inner ear to detect them.

The inner ear

One part of the inner ear is divided into three semicircular canals and helps with balance. The other part is coiled and filled with liquid, tiny hairs and nerve endings. Vibrations move through the liquid and make the hairs vibrate. When this happens the hairs touch nerves, which then send tiny electrical currents called nerve impulses to the brain and we hear a sound.

Ear trumpet

In the past, before modern hearing aids, people with poor hearing used ear trumpets to help them hear. The sound waves were collected by the opening of the trumpet and reflected off its walls down into the auditory canal. The extra sound waves reaching the eardrum made it vibrate more strongly.

An ear trumpet works in the same way as cupping your hand to your ear. It increases the size of the outer ear which helps you to hear better.

Before electrical hearing aids were invented people used ear trumpets.

Sensitive ears

Andy, Sanjay and Emma tested the sensitivity of their ears by seeing how far they could move a watch away from their ears before they could not hear it ticking. Here are their results.

Person	Left ear (cm)	Right ear (cm)
Andy	25	20
Sanjay	16	18
Emma	27	28

1 Who had the most sensitive ears?

2 Who had the least sensitive ears?

3 Whose ears had the greatest difference in sensitivity?

QUIETEN DOWN

What do you do when you hear a very loud sound? You put your hands over your ears. How does it make the sound quieter? We use a range a materials to quieten unwanted sounds.

Covering your ears

When you cover your ears, sound waves pass from the air to your hands. The waves use up energy as they pass through your hands and the waves reaching the air in your ears have smaller heights and produce a quieter sound. Ear protectors reduce the volume of the sound in a similar way.

The material in this workman's ear protectors absorbs some of the energy in sound waves and reduces the loudness of the sound reaching his ears.

Materials like glass stop sounds of speech passing through so you cannot tell what people are saying.

Reducing loudness

The loud sounds from an object can be reduced by wrapping the object in a thick material. The loud sounds with high waves leave the object, pass through a small amount of air around the object and then enter the material. As the waves pass through the material, some of their energy is used up. When the sound waves leave the material the height of their waves is reduced and they make a quieter sound.

Testing materials

Two main causes of loud sounds are voices and music. You can test how materials absorb their sounds by using a battery-powered radio as a sound source. Set the radio to a programme where people are talking. At the beginning of the experiment put the sound source on the ground and sit a distance of about two metres from it. Listen to the sound, then wrap the sound source in one layer of material and listen again. The sound should be a little quieter. Predict what will happen when you add another layer. Wrap a second layer and listen again. This experiment can be repeated with different materials to find out which is the best sound insulator.

Now set the radio to a music programme and repeat the experiment. You should find the volume of the music is not reduced as much as the volume of the speech.

Wrapping a radio in an insulating material, such as bubble wrap, will help to reduce the noise coming from it.

Comparing materials

Three different materials were wrapped around a buzzer in turn and the distance was recorded at which its sound could not be heard. The table shows the results.

Material	Distance (cm)
A	50
B	75
C	30

1 Which material was the best sound insulator and which was the worst?

2 What do you think would have been the result if an extra layer of material was used?

PITCH OF SOUNDS

A whistle makes a high-pitch sound. Thunder makes a low-pitch sound. Every sound has a pitch. It is related to the frequency of its sound wave.

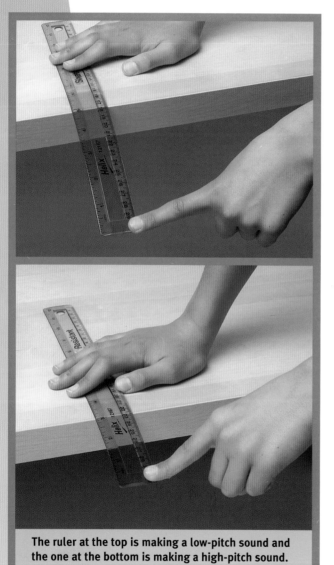

The ruler at the top is making a low-pitch sound and the one at the bottom is making a high-pitch sound.

Low frequency, low pitch

When a long length of ruler is twanged on the edge of a table, the ruler vibrates quite slowly. As only a few sound waves are produced in a certain time, we say that the waves have a low frequency. They make a sound with a low pitch.

High frequency, high pitch

When a short length of ruler is twanged on the edge of a table, the ruler vibrates very quickly. As a large number of sound waves are produced in a certain time we say that the waves have a high frequency. They make a sound with a high pitch.

The frequency

When an object vibrates, it produces many sound waves every second. The number of waves it produces each second is called the frequency of the sound. The frequency of sound waves are measured in units called hertz (Hz).

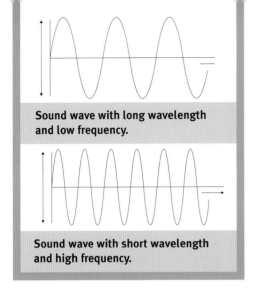

Sound wave with long wavelength and low frequency.

Sound wave with short wavelength and high frequency.

Frequency and wavelength

If the length of a sound wave is long, only a few wavelengths can pass you in a second. This means sounds with long wavelengths have a low frequency. If the wavelengths are short, a large number can pass you in a second and the sound has a high frequency.

A dog's ear can hear sounds between 67 and 45,000 Hz. This means it can hear much higher-pitched sounds than us.

The ear and frequency

The human ear can hear sounds which range in frequency from about 20 Hz to 20,000 Hz. Sounds which have a frequency below 20 Hz are called infrasounds and sounds which have a frequency above 20,000 Hz are called ultrasounds.

How much can your pets hear?

Here is a table showing the approximate range of hearing of some common pets.

1 Which animal has the greatest range of hearing?
2 Which animal has the smallest range of hearing?
3 Which pets can hear a sound of frequency 75 Hz?

Pet	Range of hearing (Hz)
Cat	45–64,000
Gerbil	100–60,000
Guinea pig	54–50,000
Rabbit	360–42,000

MUSICAL SOUNDS

Musical sounds are called notes. They are made by musical instruments and each note has a certain pitch with a different frequency. When a piece of music is played the musicians play the notes which makes sounds that are pleasant to hear.

An orchestra has four sections – one for each type of musical instrument.

Musical instruments

There are four kinds of musical instrument. They are percussion, stringed, wind and brass instruments and you can read about them on pages 22–25.

Notes and scales

There are many symbols for musical notes. We shall use an oval (see below).

Notes are written down on manuscript paper, which has groups of five lines, called staves, ruled across the pages. Musical notes are named after the following letters A, B, C, D, E, F and G. If the notes are arranged in an order where the pitch of the next note is higher than the previous note they form a scale like the one shown in the diagram below.

The notes in a musical scale are placed on and between the lines on a stave. An extra line is written through the note that is below the stave.

Melody and rhythm

The melody of a piece of music is produced by the way that the notes are arranged on the stave. In the arrangement the notes may increase and decrease in pitch without going up and down a whole scale. The rhythm of a piece of music can be thought of as the beat of the music.

For example, you can make one rhythm by tapping your foot once then clapping your hands once as you say 1, 2. You can make another rhythm by tapping your foot once and clapping your hands twice as you say 1, 2, 3. Most percussion instruments provide rhythm.

Music can be made without instruments by simply singing and clapping.

A scale of notes

Here are the frequencies of seven notes in a scale: 440, 392, 349, 262, 494, 330, 294.

1 Arrange the frequencies in the order that they are arranged in the scale.

2 The note with the lowest frequency is C. What are the other notes and their frequencies?

3 The next note in the scale is also C but it has a frequency of 524. How does this frequency compare with the frequency of the C lower in the scale?

BEATING, SCRAPING AND PLUCKING

A percussion instrument can be struck, scraped or rattled. Stringed instruments can be scraped or plucked.

Scrapers and rattlers

A guiro is made from a gourd, a vegetable like a pumpkin, which has grooves cut in it. A stick is scraped across the grooves to make the sound. A maraca is traditionally a gourd which contains dried beans. It is shaken to make a sound.

Maracas can provide a steady beat to some music.

Drums

A drum has a skin stretched across a hoop. The skin can be made of an animal skin or plastic. There are screws around the edge of the hoop which can be turned to change the tightness of the skin. If the tightness is increased the pitch of the drum is raised. If the tightness is reduced the pitch of the drum is lowered. The loudness of a drum depends on the size of the force used to strike it. If the drum is hit hard it will make a loud sound but if it is tapped it will make a quieter sound.

The tightness of a kettle drum skin can be changed quickly with a foot pedal to make a range of different notes.

Xylophone

A xylophone has a number of wooden or metal bars. When each one is hit, it produces a musical note. The whole range of bars produce a musical scale. This means that the xylophone can be used to play a tune.

Strings and elastic bands

The strings on musical instruments behave in a similar way to elastic bands. If they are stretched and then plucked, they vibrate. The vibrations produce a sound of a particular frequency. If they are stretched a little more and plucked they produced a sound of a higher pitch or frequency. If they are slackened a little and plucked they produce a sound of a lower pitch or frequency.

The pitch or frequency of the sound produced by an elastic band or a string depends on its length and thickness. A long string produces a sound with a lower frequency than the sound produced by a short string. A thick string produces a sound with a higher frequency than the sound produced by a thin string.

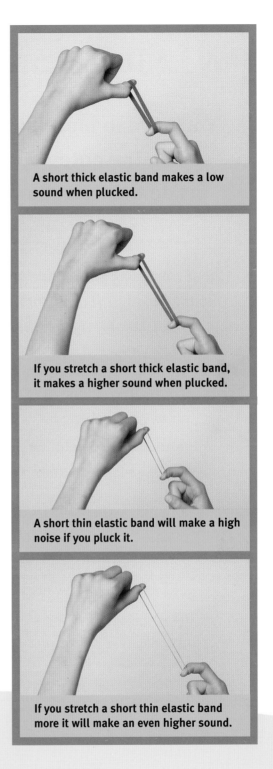

A short thick elastic band makes a low sound when plucked.

If you stretch a short thick elastic band, it makes a higher sound when plucked.

A short thin elastic band will make a high noise if you pluck it.

If you stretch a short thin elastic band more it will make an even higher sound.

Drum pitch

Here are the diameters and pitches (frequencies) of four drums:

A 20 cm – 200 Hz
B 8 cm – 400 Hz
C 30 cm – 120 Hz
D 15 cm – 300 Hz

1 Arrange the drums in order of size starting with the smallest.

2 How does the size of the drum affect the pitch of the note it plays?

WIND INSTRUMENTS

You have to blow into a wind instrument to make a sound. The note you produce is due to the air inside the instrument vibrating.

Straws and pan pipes

If you take a straw and carefully blow across the top of it, you will make the air inside the straw vibrate. The vibrating air makes the straw vibrate, too, and it makes a note.

If you cut a couple of centimetres off one end of the straw and blow again, you make a higher pitched note. This is due to the shorter straw making a shorter sound wave.

Pan pipes are made from wooden or plastic tubes with different lengths. The lengths of the tubes have been made so that when you blow across them you make a musical scale and can play a tune on them.

Each pipe produces a note when air is blown across the top of it.

Notes and frequency

A pan pipe was made with tubes of the following lengths: 15 cm, 14 cm, 12 cm, 10 cm and 9 cm. Here are some frequencies of sounds produced by the tubes – 440, 262, 392, 294, 330 Hz.

1 What was the frequency of the sound produced by each tube?
2 Find the note produced by each pipe by looking at your answers to the panel on page 21.

The recorder

The recorder is a tube with holes in it.
If you cover some of the holes with your fingers and thumb then blow, you produce a note of a certain pitch.

If you change the number of holes you cover and blow again the pitch of the note changes. This is due to the wavelength of the vibrating air in the recorder changing when you change the number of holes you cover.

By changing the position of your fingers over the holes on the recorder, you can play a tune.

Making the air vibrate

When you blow into a recorder, the air passes quickly over a slot and this makes it start to vibrate. Musicians who play brass wind instruments, such as the trumpet, blow a 'raspberry' into the instrument. Their lips vibrate when they do this, making the air vibrate. Some instruments, such as the clarinet, have a thin piece of material called a reed. When the musician blows into the instrument the reed vibrates and makes the air in the instrument vibrate.

The vibrations of a wind instrument are transmitted to the air at its open end. If the end is covered, as in this picture, the volume of sound is greatly reduced.

SPEED OF SOUND

If you stood close to someone as they used a large hammer to knock in a post, you would see and hear the hammer strike the post at the same time. If you stood 150 metres away, something odd would happen. You would see the hammer strike the post and hear the thud afterwards. This is because sound travels more slowly than light.

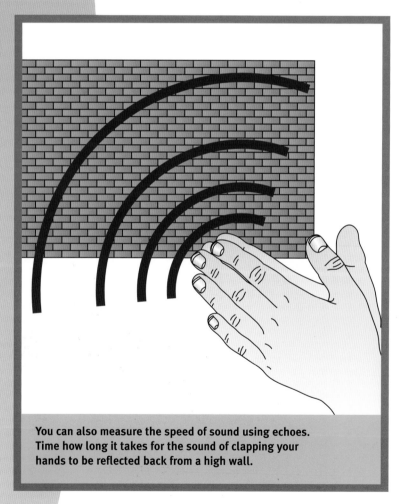

You can also measure the speed of sound using echoes. Time how long it takes for the sound of clapping your hands to be reflected back from a high wall.

Measuring the speed of sound in air

This simple experiment can be used to measure the speed of sound. A distance of about 150 metres is measured out between the source of the sound and the observer. When sound is seen to be made, by clapping together two pieces of wood for example, the observer sets a stopwatch and records the time until the sound is heard. The speed of sound is found by recording how long it took the sound to travel the distance from the sound source. The speed of sound in air at 20 °C is 343 metres per second.

Travelling faster than sound

Some jet aircraft can travel faster than sound. When the aircraft is travelling below the speed of sound, the sound it makes spreads out as waves in front of it and you can hear it approaching. When the aircraft reaches the speed of sound, the waves do not move away in front of it but gather and form a shock wave. As the aircraft flies faster than the speed of sound it breaks through the shock wave and leaves it behind. This means that when the aircraft passes you it does so in silence then the shock wave arrives and makes a loud roar called a sonic boom.

Sound lags behind an aircraft flying at supersonic speed and makes a loud bang after the aircraft has passed.

Sound and temperature

The graph shows the speed of sound at different temperatures.

1 At what temperature is the speed of sound 340 m/s?

2 What is the speed of sound at 20°C?

3 How does the speed of sound change as the temperature rises?

4 Predict the speed of sound at 30 °C. Use your finger to follow the line of the graph to 30°C, then look down to see the speed of sound.

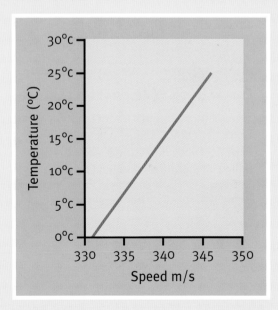

CAN YOU REMEMBER THE ESSENTIALS?

Here are the essential science facts about changing sounds. They are set out in the order you can read about them in the book. Spend a couple of minutes learning each set of facts. If you can learn them all, you will know all the essentials about changing sounds.

Vibrations
(pages 6-7)

A vibrating object moves quickly up and down or from side to side.
Vibrations make sounds.
Vibrations can be felt.
When a tuning fork vibrates it makes a musical note.
Vibrating objects produce waves in the material around it.

Sound waves (pages 10-11)

The four parts of a wave are the crest, trough, amplitude and wavelength.
Vibrating objects possess movement energy.
Energy is used up as a wave passes through a material.
Sound waves are reflected from the surfaces they strike.
An echo is caused by reflected sound waves.
Energy is used to make sound waves.

Sound on the move (pages 8-9)

Sounds travel through air (and other gases), water (and other liquids) and solids.
There is a vacuum in space.
Sound cannot travel through space.

Loud and quiet sounds
(pages 12-13)

The loudness of sounds is measured in decibels.
The symbol for decibel is dB.
Sound waves with a large height produce loud sounds.
Sound waves with a small height produce quiet sounds.

The ear (pages 14–15)

The ear has three parts: the outer, middle and inner ear.

The outer ear collects sound waves which cause the eardrum to vibrate.

The middle ear strengthens the vibrations and passes them to the inner ear.

The inner ear changes the vibrations into electrical currents, which pass to the brain.

In the past, an ear trumpet was used by deaf people to gather more sound waves for the ear.

Quieten down (pages 16–17)

Materials can be wrapped around objects making loud sounds to make the sounds quieter.

The sound of speech is more greatly reduced than the sound of music by using materials to quieten sound.

The best sound insulator can be found by wrapping samples of different materials around an object producing a loud sound.

Pitch of sound (pages 18–19)

The pitch of a sound is due to the frequency of the sound waves.

Low-frequency sounds have long wavelengths.

High-frequency sounds have short wavelengths.

The frequency of a sound is measured in hertz (Hz).

Musical sounds (pages 20–21)

Each note has a certain pitch.

A group of notes arranged in the order of their pitch is called a scale.

There are four different kinds of musical instruments: percussion, string, wind and brass.

The beat of a piece of music is played by percussion instruments.

Beating, scraping and plucking (pages 22–23)

Percussion instruments are struck, scraped or rattled.

The pitch of a drum depends on the tightness of its skin.

The loudness of a drum depends on how hard it is struck.

Stringed instruments are scraped or plucked.

The pitch of a vibrating string depends on its length, thickness and how much it is stretched.

Wind instruments (pages 24–25)

Air is blown through a wind instrument to make a sound.

The note is made by air vibrating in the instrument.

Brass wind instruments are played by blowing a raspberry into them.

Speed of sound (pages 26–27)

Sound travels more slowly than light.

The speed of sound is found by recording how long it took the sound to travel a certain distance from its source.

Aircraft which travel faster than sound produce a sonic boom.

GLOSSARY

Balance The ability of the body to stay upright and not fall over.

Battery A small device which holds electricity.

Cartilage A tough but flexible material produced by the body, sometimes called gristle.

Cymbal A circular, slightly concave, plate made of brass or bronze which is struck with a stick to make a musical sound.

Echo The second sound produced when the first sound is reflected from a distant surface.

Energy Something which allows an object or a living thing to take part in an activity.

Frequency The number of sound waves that pass a place in a second.

Gas A substance which does not have any shape or size.

Infrasounds Sounds that have frequencies of less than 20 Hz

Microscope An instrument which gives a highly magnified view of a tiny object.

Nerves Long thin structures inside the body which carry electrical signals (called nerve impulses) between the brain and other parts of the body.

Orchestra A large group of musicians who play wind, stringed and percussion instruments.

Oscilloscope An instrument which enables the wave made by vibrations to be examined.

Percussion instruments Musical instruments that are struck to make a sound.

Solid A substance which has a fixed shape and size.

Steel A shiny metal made from iron which is used for making a wide range of objects from pins to car bodies.

Stringed instruments Musical instruments that have a number of strings which can be plucked, as with a guitar, or scraped, as on a violin.

Supersonic Faster than sound.

Vacuum A completely empty space. It does not contain any of the three forms of matter – solid, liquid or gas.

Ultrasounds Sounds which have frequencies of more than 20,000 Hz.

Wavelength The length of a wave measured from one crest to the next, or one trough to the next.

Wind instrument A musical instrument that is played by blowing into it.

Xylophone An instrument made from a row of wooden or metal bars of different lengths. The bars are hit with a hammer to make a sound.

ANSWERS

What is sound? (pages 6–7)

1 Hit C.

2 Hit B.

3 Hit C.

Sound on the move (pages 8–9)

1 It speeds up.

2 4500 m/ seconds faster.

Sound waves (pages 10–11)

1 A

2 C

3 B

4 B

Loud and quiet sounds (pages 12–13)

2 This will depend on individual circumstances.

The ear (pages 14–15)

1 Emma.

2 Sanjay.

3 Andy.

Quieten down (pages 16–17)

1 C was the best sound insulator and B was the worst.

2 The sound would have been reduced and the distance at which you could hear it would also be reduced.

Pitch of sounds (pages 18–19)

1 Cat

2 Rabbit

3 Guinea pig and cat

Musical sounds (pages 20–21)

1 262, 294, 330, 349, 392, 440, 494.

2 D = 294, E = 330, F = 349, G =392, A = 440, B =494.

3 It is twice the frequency of the lower C.

Beating, scraping and plucking (pages 22–23)

1 B, D, A, C.

2 The larger the drum the lower its pitch.

Wind instruments (pages 24–25)

1 15 cm = 262, 14 cm = 294, 12 cm = 330, 10 cm = 392, 9 cm = 440.

2 15 cm = C, 14 cm = D, 12 cm = E, 10 cm = G, 9 cm = A.

Speed of sound (pages 26–27)

1 15°C.

2 343 m/s.

3 It increases steadily.

4 349 m/s.

INDEX